Leland W. Howe, Ph.D.

taking charge of your life

Argus
Communications

A Division of **DLM**, Inc.
Niles, Illinois 60648 U.S.A.

Library of Congress Catalog Card Number: 77-86340
International Standard Book Number: 0-913592-93-5

Argus Communications
A Division of **DLM,** Inc.
7440 Natchez Avenue
Niles, IL 60648 U.S.A.

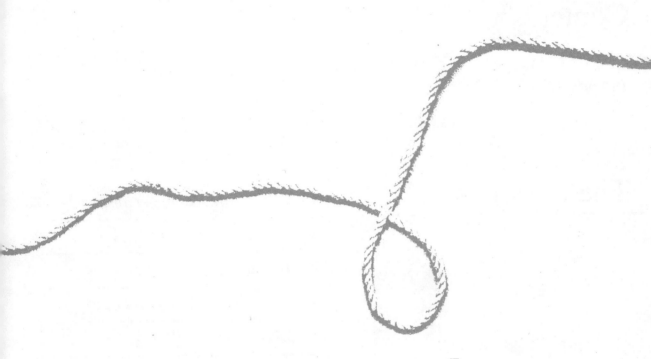

To
Mary Martha

Contents

The exercises

Introduction

Hi. Excuse the familiarity, but this is a very personal book. As you begin reading it, I think that you will soon agree that it is not only personal—but it's about you. I wish I could sit down with you and talk. But that can't be so right now. So, I thought that the next best thing would be for me to imagine that you are sitting across from me and that we are having a person-to-person talk. Let's begin, shall we? You are the one that begins—and because you are important, you are the one speaking in letters like these.

SUCCESS. For a long time I didn't think about it one way or the other. Then, I made a mental list—there's our family doctor, our son's teacher, the man who runs the bank, the local woman who is a famous painter, the judge, my high school coach, an old girl friend who is now an opera star, the television announcer next door, the airline pilot—all these people and many more are happy and successful. They are leaders in their field. They seem to be doing well and doing what they set out to do.

Were they born successful?

And, what about the other people? The ones I see that just seem to drift along at a job they do because it's there? A job they don't really like or enjoy. Yet, they keep on doing it, for years.

Were they born drifters?

And how about the ones that seem to give up or quit trying. They seem to think they are beaten before they start. What's wrong with them? Why don't they take charge of their lives and go after what they want? Or were they born failures?

Congratulations! By observing, thinking and asking these questions, you've just taken the first, most important step in taking charge of your own life.

You're right, of course. Nobody is simply born to be successful or to be a failure. The successful people have made themselves successful. They have discovered something very important— that it is up to each person to take the responsibility for what happens to her or him, to make things happen. They have learned that each of us is really in charge of our own behavior, that it is not enough to just drift along with the crowd, waiting for something good to happen, blaming others for putting us into a role in life that we do not really want to play. To them, living is a challenge, filled with purpose and meaning.

But so many people fail to live life this way. Why? Don't they have the skills to succeed?

That's only part of it. You do have to have skills. In a way, living is like a game of baseball. You can't play well unless you know how to bat, catch, and throw the ball. In life you can't "play" well unless you know how to speak, listen, organize, and get along with other people. But, you can learn to do these things— if only you make yourself get out there and practice what you know you need to learn. It isn't lack of skills which keeps most people off the playing field of life. It is something *inside them*. People are their own worst enemies.

ENEMIES? INSIDE? You make it sound like there's a war going on.

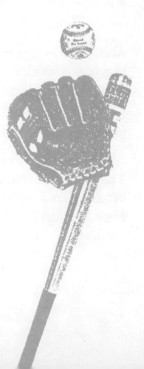

8

Well, in a way there is. There is a "bright" side in each of us that wants to get out there and play, to be the best, to succeed, to be a winner. But, there is another side in most of us that is afraid to compete. It is the voice in *your* head—in almost everybody's head—that tells you that you are a loser, that you are not smart enough, or quick enough to make it. Then, the bright side comes back and says, "nonsense, you are just as good as everyone else," that you are not stupid or slow. The problem is that failure puts the bright side on the defensive so that the dark side keeps on saying, "I told you so." That's when you give up and quit trying. But the bright side never quits trying to convince you, deep down inside, that you can succeed.

▶ **You mean the bright side never dies, it just fades away?**

Something like that. It's still there trying to get back in charge.

▶ **How do you know that?**

I've seen it happen over and over again. Take a person who has just about given up on life. Tell him that you know he is worthwhile and that he can be successful. At first he won't believe you because you are saying something his dark or "not ok" side won't accept. His "not ok" side will fight you every inch of the way, but if you really mean it, and you can see and point out something worthwhile about the person, you will begin to see a dramatic change. He will begin to act differently—to respect himself a little. Deep down inside you have restored some authority to his good voice. He begins to listen to it telling him that he can be successful after all. Keep feeding that bright side and sooner or later the dark side will go on the defensive and eventually it will be the one that fades away.

▶ That sounds almost too easy and simple. There must be a catch somewhere.

It is easy and simple but you are right—there is a catch. And, the catch is that there are not enough people to listen to all the people whose "not ok" sides are in charge. You see, most of us are in the same boat. When our "not ok" is talking or shouting, as the case usually is, our bright side is so busy defending itself that we don't have the energy to take time out and help other people listen to their own bright side. So there we are, each of us stuck on our own little desert island, busy defending ourselves from this "not ok" side that wants to keep us down, to feed on us like a vulture.

▶ You mean it's hopeless then?

No—I didn't say that. It's far from hopeless, but you have to realize that each of us has to face up to this vulture which wants to convince us that we are hopeless and worthless. It's important to know that you are not the only one who is being attacked in this way.

▶ Where did this vulture come from anyway? I know I have one because I do hear myself telling myself that I'm not smart enough, or good enough, just as you say. But why do I do it?

The main reason is that we were all little once. Children are helpless when born and they aren't very smart and they knock things over and make messes of themselves and everything around them. Some children were lucky—they had parents (and brothers, sisters, grandparents, aunts, and uncles), who knew that babies and young children do such things, who loved them, and who never rejected them, or called them stupid. And some children had friends in school, and teachers, who loved them and never made fun of or called them names even when their noses were running and their baby teeth were coming out, and they looked stupid and awkward.

But most people aren't that lucky. Now, I don't want to sound like I'm against mothers or fathers, or that I'm down on grandparents and friends, because I'm not. It really wasn't their fault—or *their* parents' fault (remember, your parents had parents, too). In fact, I don't think it is really anybody's fault that we all get angry and frustrated and yell and make critical remarks about each other. Everyone is doing the best they can, given their situation, but there simply isn't enough love and affection to go around. So, most of us get trampled a bit and never get over feeling that we are helpless, not very smart, and not very attractive.

▶ **So, we are still sort of stuck back there in childhood somewhere?**

That's it. Let's say that you are still angry at your mom for not hugging you enough, and at dad for giving you that spanking, and at your second grade teacher for putting tape over your mouth and making you sit in the corner. You may still be feeling sorry for yourself because you dropped your birthday cake off the tray while your mom was taking a picture of you when you turned five, and for losing the class election in the sixth grade. You may still be afraid of the dark because your Uncle Pete told you scarey stories when you weren't able to sort it all out. And, then some really bad things happened to you that should never happen to anyone—like when your grandmother died—

▶ Yes, I know the sort of things you mean.

O.K. All of us have that sort of pain in our past, all added up and stored away for instant use to prove to us that we aren't good enough. There is seldom a day or even an hour when something that someone says or does, or fails to say or do cannot remind us of one of these painful events from our past. Nobody likes to re-live such things. So, after a while you learn that it's easier to shut it all out by watching television or through busy-work.

▶ It's beginning to sound hopeless again. But it's not, right?

Hooray! That's your bright side working again. There certainly is hope. I'm not going into all of this to depress you. But it's important to know where those vultures come from, just like it's important to know that practically everybody has one in their head. But, you don't have to let the vultures eat you alive, and you don't have to remain stuck back there in your childhood feeling helpless for the rest of your life. You can get unhooked, get free and start moving on your own. But first you have to know what the problems are and want to get rid of them. The first step is simply to say to yourself, "I'm sick and tired of being this way. I'm going to do something about it." When you've made that choice, you've won half the battle.

▶ I'm sure that's easier said than done.

Yes of course, it would be much easier to have someone come along every few minutes and tell you that you are smart, attractive, and capable. That would be nice but it won't happen.

The way to make it happen is to learn to be your own best friend—*you* come along every five minutes and tell yourself how great you are.

▶ That sounds kind of nutty.

Perhaps, but I happen to know it works. First, think of something that you are good at. Don't think of the negative side—that you can't do it as well as so-and-so. Think only of the positive side—that you can do it and are good at it.

▶ Well, I'm pretty good at. . .ping-pong. . .or is that too silly?

Not at all. It's a game that takes coordination, good reflexes, quick thinking. So pay yourself a compliment about your ping-pong game. Don't be embarrassed—do it, say it to yourself.

▶ I'm pretty good at playing ping-pong.

Fine, but don't qualify it. That's the vulture in you trying to pick away at your bright side. Phrases like "pretty good" and "some of the time" and "I think I'm not bad at. . ." are back-sliders. Lock that vulture in a cage and throw away the key. Now try it once more.

▶ I'm good at playing ping-pong.

Great. Now keep saying it until you really believe it. It may take a while.

▶ But I know I don't play ping-pong as well as my friend.

There's the vulture, rattling the cage. Tell him to be quiet. Life is not one big contest. It's a struggle at times, to be sure, but most of the time you have to get along with, work with other people. There isn't now and never has been a person who has the skills, knowledge, or strength to make it completely on his or her own without help from others. So, forget the "I've got to do it better than my friend" stuff. Sure he's good, but that doesn't mean you're not good, too. There will always be somebody who can do something better. The mistake is to let your whole idea of what you are worth get tied up in comparisons. Because when someone else does do something better than you do, it makes you feel like you are worth nothing.

▶ **But isn't the measure of my self-worth what I can do?**

Definitely not. Stop rating yourself in terms of others. You were born with self-worth. Now find out what you are good at. You have not even begun to achieve your full potential. And it is because you don't appreciate your self-worth. OK, so you are a poor speller. Does that make you less worthwhile than the best speller in town? A very silly idea, but one that most people get trapped into holding. So do your best at what you do, and appreciate yourself for it. It's the way up and out.

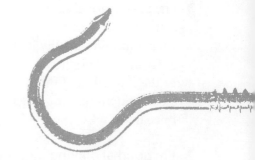

▶ **O.K. I've got it. Now what else can I do to get unhooked?**

Hold it! Don't be in such a rush to get away from the good part of you. After all, you've just succeeded at something here. Take a minute and bask in your own sunshine. Most people are too quick to put themselves down and tell themselves how awful they are. But when they do accomplish something, they don't stop and dwell on it nearly as long as they do on those ancient put-downs. And, they should. . .you should. Every day. It is one of the most important ways to learn to take care of yourself—your bright side.

▶ I hadn't thought of it that way. I mean, I know enough to get enough sleep and to eat the right food. But to spend time appreciating myself? I didn't think I needed to do that, or that it would be O.K. to do that because it sounds like a person who is stuck on himself.

That's what too many people think. It's a vulture trick to keep you down. Personally, I'd rather risk being a little self-centered than thinking of myself as a loser. Some self-appreciation instead of self put-downs would do all of us more good than harm.

▶ Now it doesn't sound so hopeless. It's beginning to make sense.

Good. But really, down deep, you've known what I've been telling you all along. It's not a matter of convincing you. It's more a matter of my sharing with you what I have found through experience working with others to be true, and you're simply realizing that it's also true for you.

O.K., you asked: "What else can I do to get unhooked?" Well, another step is to begin to tune into your basic human needs—not for just food and water and shelter, but your inside needs.

Do you know that when I ask most people what they have done for *themselves* today, most of them can't tell me a single thing. Or if I ask them how much time they have devoted to themselves today they just look puzzled.

People are so busy working, studying, cooking, cleaning, running errands—that they manage to get through whole days—most days—without spending any time on themselves.

But people have "inside" needs—psychological needs for such things as healthy servings of affection, belonging, privacy, respect, praise, pleasure, and a lot more. These needs are just as basic and vital as our need for food and water. If you don't satisfy these needs sooner or later you burn yourself down to the point of collapse and exhaustion. In fact, that's what we have far too much of today—burned out people who can't think or feel or enjoy life because they are psychologically exhausted.

▶ **I'm afraid I have to plead guilty to that. I've been trying to think of something I did for myself today and—nothing!**

You're in plenty of company. But you can change things around very simply. Just take an hour, or a half hour—even ten minutes will help—and reserve them for your own private use each day. Use the reserved time to do something that you like and which gives you real satisfaction—inside. That's the first step in learning to take care of yourself. Watch what happens to you. You will have more energy and—unless I'm wrong—you will find yourself smiling more often, too.

As a next step, do some thinking about what your needs are. More companionship, more affection, more privacy? Write them down where you can see them. Give some time to thinking how you can arrange your life to meet those needs. Decide what you need to ask, and then *ask*.

▶ **You mean ask for what I need?**

Is that such a shocking idea? It seems never to dawn on people that they should ask for what they need. No, somehow your family and friends are all supposed to be mind readers and know what you need and want. And when they don't, your feelings are hurt, you feel put-down, worthless. And, there you are back in the same old rut, the same vicious circle, the one that seems to ground around and around and down and down.

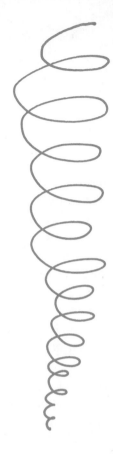

▶ Yes, it certainly does.

Well, it doesn't have to be that way. Not if you ask for what you need. It is the best way to fill those needs, and it will save you a lot of needless negative thinking and several thousand miles of hurt feelings.

And, don't just ask when you happen to think of it. Keep that list of needs where you can see it and make a schedule for the week that will guarantee that all of them get met.

▶ I'm sure this will work for many people, but what if I have trouble doing it alone? Does everything have to depend on me?

It's not unusual to have trouble doing things alone. If you need help from someone, get it. The point is that you just can't sit around waiting for someone to come along and fill your needs. It simply may not happen and it will never happen often enough to be of real help.

But, this is just what many people do. Sit and wait for that perfect person, who will come along and take care of their inner needs for the rest of their lives. And most people never find that perfect person. You can test the truth of this by looking at the statistics on divorce in this country.

The reality is that there is no one perfect person who has been put into the world to take care of you and all of your needs. If there is any approach to this sort of person, it is probably in the form of your parents, for a few years while you were very young. But even parents can't be perfect.

You might as well face it. No one can take care of you. You have to do it yourself. Which is not to say that you don't need the Help and support of others, or that they don't need your help and support—but you have to take the main load, the main responsibility.

So throw out the idea of waiting, of hoping or looking for that perfect person, that super mom or dad who will take care of little you for all time. Get up off the seat of your pants and get out there and let others know that you want them to have faith in you, to give you some support.

Now, obviously, I don't mean that you should walk up to somebody and say, "Hey, how about giving me some support?"—although even that would be better than just sitting around waiting. What I suggest is a much more indirect but workable approach. Pick out a person you know and would like to get to know better—somebody you could offer some support of your own and who wouldn't think it too strange that you care about them. Think about some ways you can give them positive support. Listen to them, respond to them, show genuine interest in them, compliment them on some real qualities that you see in them. You can't fake this interest and support because people have built-in radar systems which will detect fakery.

What will happen is that as you tune into and affirm the bright side of this person, he will begin to feel better about himself. His vulture will get back inside its cage, and he will suddenly have more freedom from his "not ok" voice, more time to be positive. In my experience, nine out of ten times the person will recognize that it is you who has helped him and respond by giving you generous amounts of that newly freed attention.

So, you have done two good things—killed two vultures with one stone: you have helped another person out of the vicious circle and in doing so, helped yourself out of your own.

This works. It has worked for me. It works because it is often easier to find good in someone else than in yourself. One day, if you are really going to get yourself unhooked, you must see the good in yourself and learn to take care of your own needs. But, if it is easier to start with a friend, by all means do just that.

> **What if the friend doesn't respond as you say and just leaves you sitting there in your own vicious circle?**

That's a chance you have to take. It could happen but the odds are against it. If it does happen you simply have to try again with another person. You have only your vulture to lose. Anyway, you should get yourself out of such a relationship that does no good for you. For instance, who needs "friends" who put you down and make you feel bad about yourself? You can do that for yourself. If you have one of these friends who specializes in putting you down and thus making himself feel superior, it is probably that you accept his judgment of the situation and are letting his vulture feed on you. Or, it may be happening the other way around—that you are making yourself feel better at the expense of another. In either case it's a bad relationship for both of you.

It is only when you treat another as an equal, have mutual respect for each other's strengths, and mutual understanding of your weaknesses that a relationship can become healthy and freedom-building for both of you. So, don't hang on to bad friendships out of habit. Such a relationship is not only bad for you, but it is blocking the road to where you want to get, taking up your time, clouding your sense of purpose.

And the same thing goes for situations and even places which keep you upset and rub your nose in the painful memories of the past. Why keep living in a house filled with constant reminders of old hurts? Why keep going to places which drag you down and make you feel worthless and awkward?

It makes much more sense to sort things out and spend your time in places and situations that you enjoy, that lift you up. Think about it and locate those trouble places—and then drop them. Experiment with finding the good places and then go there, do those things you find uplifting. As you make the change from negative to positive, you will notice that increase in energy we talked about, the beginning of the jolt that will shoot you into the constructive circle.

> **Hey! I'm feeling more energy already. I'm ready to get at it.**

Good! But just one more thought—as you begin to succeed at what you try, you will feel more purpose and satisfaction come into your life. But it won't automatically bring you the happiness you also seek. This comes only as you develop a clear-cut direction for your life and then begin moving ahead, fully in charge of every step of the way.

This is where some good old-fashioned thinking is needed. There is no substitute for it, no magic formula. It means asking yourself questions like:

"What do I really want out of life? For myself? For others?"

"What is worth living for?"

"What are my values?"

"Which life goals will be most satisfying to me personally? Most socially constructive for others?"

When you have answers to these questions—and it will take time to clarify them—you will be on your way to both satisfaction and happiness.

So now, you know some of the specific things you can do to get unhooked, to put your life on the track toward being fully effective, happy, and successful. I've gone pretty fast with the words so to help make these ideas clear and practical, I've put together, in the following pages, a group of exercises which can help you or anyone who is willing to do them. The exercises can really help you put more purpose and meaning into your life by encouraging you to explore your goals, needs, strengths, and ways of gaining support. They are tested steps to get you up and going, to realizing and then moving toward taking charge of your life instead of waiting for things to simply happen to you.

▶ Well, wish me luck. I'm ready to begin.

You don't need luck. Everything you need to be the sort of person you want to be is already inside you. You just need to start believing it. If you do become the person you want to be after reading and working your way through this book, don't thank me.

Thank yourself, because you did it. You're in charge.

Purpose of the exercises

Relax. I wish I could call them something that didn't sound so much like work. Think of them more as games with a purpose. But exercises is really the right word—they are designed to work like physical exercises, only to build up the muscles of your bright or positive side. There are seventeen main exercises with four more grouped under certain headings—twenty-one in all. Specifically, these exercises will help you to learn to:

1. Identify and increase your strengths, talents, and abilities.

This is important because your continued growth depends very much upon having strong roots: the more strengths, talents and abilities you have—and know you have—the better you will grow and succeed.

2. Identify your past and present successes, achievements, and accomplishments—and to plan more in the future.

This is important because the actual success and fullness of your life is actually determined by the feelings—the attitude—you take in the beginning about your ability to succeed, to achieve, and to accomplish things.

3. Identify the sources of your support and nourishment.

This is important because you cannot grow and develop without "inner food"—in a vacuum. Like all living things, human beings need tender loving care. If you spend time with friends and family, and in situations where you get attention, affection, and support, your growth will be nourished. If you do not, your growth may well be stunted.

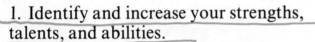

4. Clarify beliefs and values.

This is important because beliefs and values give direction to your growth. There is no insurance plan that guarantees that human beings grow in the right direction—it is quite possible to grow in the wrong way unless you stop and examine what you believe in and value from time to time—and where you are headed.

5. Set and achieve personal goals for your present and future growth.

This is important because good intentions are not enough. You can learn to direct and take charge of your own growth in life. Learning how to set and achieve your own goals is a vital part of this process.

How to use the exercises

Each of the exercises is designed to be self-explanatory. Simply read and follow the directions for each exercise. If you are doing them with the help of a teacher or workshop leader, you will want to follow his or her directions in going through the exercises.

Validation scavenger hunt

To

Help you develop
an awareness
of your strengths,
talents,
and abilities.

There's a big party. People need to be entertained. Let them entertain themselves. Guests are divided into teams and given lists of things to go out and find. Strange things, ordinary things, rare things, cheap things—from bailing wire to guppies—as many as can be begged, borrowed, or found in an hour or so. A team spreads out with a plan: knocks on doors, searches alleys, makes phone calls, ransacks their own houses. They seldom find everything on the impossible list but it is amazing how many strange items are actually turned up, as if by magic, out of nowhere with a little (or a lot of) imagination and cooperation. Scavenger hunts are fun. They restore faith in the art of thinking, in the skills of looking, in the virtues of imagination. Everyday things suddenly seem to take on a new value. Looking. . .seeking. . .can be rewarding. It gets you out of the rut. And you may find something to value, especially about yourself!

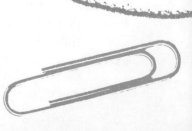

To do

Go on a scavenger hunt. Your task on the scavenger hunt is to find several things that are symbolic or remind you of three of your strengths, talents, or abilities. For example, let's say you find a stone which reminds you of your ability to stand firm (like a rock) by your convictions even under great pressure from others to change; or a flower which reminds you of your sensitivity and gentleness. Try looking around your house, in the park, on the school grounds, or in the classroom. When you return, write in the space on page 26 what you found and what strength, talent, or abilities each represents.

Why do

Sometimes it is difficult to simply sit down and list our strengths, talents, and abilities. The scavenger hunt helps to make this task easier as well as enjoyable since the things we find serve to remind us of our good points.

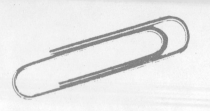

Do

object	strength, talent, or ability it presents

1. _____

2. _____

3. _____

4. _____

5. _____

More to do

Like a tree, we have weathered and endured many a bad storm in our lives. Maybe it was the time our pet rabbit died, or when we lost the championship game, or when we broke up with our boyfriend or girlfriend. It hurt and perhaps left a scar or two, but our inner strength pulled us through.

Make a list of the storms in your life—the times when you were troubled or upset—then list the strength(s) or ability(ies) that helped get you through. Here are some possibilities:

my self-confidence

my religious faith

my faith in others

my reasoning power

my cheerfulness

my hard work

my courage

my honesty

my competitiveness

my love

my stability

my inner security

my aggressiveness

my independence

my loyalty to others

my open-mindedness

my flexibility

my commitment to my values

my commitment to others

my acceptance of others

my empathy with others

my self-discipline

my acceptance of events

my creativity

my physical endurance

Mirror, Mirror...

To

Further build
and reinforce
your feelings
of self-worth
and importance.

Down through history many myths and superstitions have been
connected with mirrors. . . .To break one, for example, was to
bring on seven years' bad luck. Vampires and other nasty types
were said not to reflect any image. Some mirrors—remember the
Wicked Queen's in *Snow White*—were supposed to be able to
know everything and be able to predict future events. Few
people believe such things today but many still feel uneasy about
what they may see if they look steadily into a good mirror. Some
see only their blemishes or weak points. If they think themselves
too fat or too skinny, too tall or too short, they would rather not
have the evidence reflected. But others love mirrors and use
them to pose and preen. The truth is that mirrors can reflect only
a tiny part of the reality about anyone. They don't show the
qualities that make you what you are. For that you need a very
special sort of mirror.

To do

Find a mirror and look into it at yourself. Say to the mirror the following words:

*Mirror, mirror. . .
Tell me what you see.
Tell me what you like
Best about me!*

Then, put the mirror to your ear and listen to its reply.* Do this five times. The first time, it should tell you what it likes best about you physically. The second time, what it likes best about you intellectually. The third time, what it likes best about you emotionally. The fourth time, what it likes best about you socially; and the fifth time, what it likes best about you morally or spiritually. Write the responses in the space provided on page 30.

*You must pretend that the mirror answers you by providing your own answer.

Why do

We have strengths and abilities in all five dimensions; physical, intellectual, emotional, social, and moral or spiritual. This activity helps to point this out as well as further build and reinforce our feelings of self-worth.

① *physical*
② *intellectual*
③ *emotional*
④ *social*
⑤ *moral/spiritual*

Do

dimension: *response:*

physical

_____

_____

_____

intellectual

_____

_____

_____

emotional

_____

_____

social

_____

_____

moral/spiritual

_____

_____

More to do

Do a self-advertisement (newspaper or magazine ad, TV or radio spot, or a billboard) which highlights your physical, intellectual, emotional, social, and/or moral/spiritual strengths and abilities.

Introducing the new improved me!

TALENT SCOUTS

To

Help you further increase your sense of self-worth and self-importance.

On a television talk show a famous movie actor told of his despair over his son's habits. The boy had done nothing since graduating from high school but stay up in his messy bedroom playing an electric guitar. He showed no interest in getting a job or furthering his education. Finally his father told him, "You're going to have to get up and get out of here. You sit around playing that thing day and night. What do you think, that some talent scout is going to walk by the house and 'discover' you?" The next day the leader of a well-known rock group was passing the house—driving in a convertible though, not walking—and heard the boy playing. He stopped his car, knocked on the door, and signed the young man up with his group on the spot.

To do

Stars, Inc., a company in the business of locating talent, has just sent a team of talent scouts to interview you. They are not interested in your weak points—these don't matter. Their interest is in your strong points—your strengths and abilities. Below is a copy of the report they file. What would you want it to say? Write it on page 34. Here are some areas you might want to include:

Why do

Identifying our strengths, talents, and abilities can help to make us feel like we are somebody important and worthwhile.

physical traits

character traits

personality traits

motor skills

thinking skills

knowledge possessed

communication skills

appearance

organizational skills

relating skills

mental abilities

physical abilities

Do

TALENT REPORT

For _____ .

_____ of

Prepared for Stars, Inc., on this _____

_____ , _____ .

We found the above named person to have the following strengths, abilities, talents, skills, and capabilities:

_____

_____

_____

_____

We highly recommend him/her to the President and Board of Directors of Stars, Inc.

      Yours respectfully,

      A. J. Cooper, Team Leader
      William Read
      Anna Williams

More to do

Make a collage of your strengths, talents, and abilities. Use old snapshots, newspaper clippings, drawings, magazine pictures, headlines, scraps of material, and anything else that you can find that represents or reminds you of your strong points.

optimism talks

victory!

My family inheritance

To

Help you become aware of the strengths, talents, and abilities that you have inherited, acquired, or learned from your family and relatives.

There was once a young woman who had devoted many years to caring for her aging aunt. Now the aunt had inherited a great deal of money from her brother, years before. But she had never spent any of it, nor even told anyone of her fortune. When she lay dying she called her niece and told her: "You have given me years of your life out of love and I want to repay you with at least a token. Take this old sweater of mine and wear it until you become rich."

The niece thanked her aunt but secretly she was hurt. "I know that aunt is not rich but if she wanted to give me a token it might at least have been her ring or her watch," she said to herself while throwing the sweater into a corner of her closet.

Soon the aunt died and several years passed before the young woman dug out the sweater one day to work in the yard. While she was raking she became aware of something in the pocket of the sweater. She found a key wrapped in a note. The paper gave her directions to and legal title to the hundred thousand dollars she found in her aunt's secret bank box.

You may never inherit so much money, but you might be surprised at the treasures that have been passed down to you, if only you'll stop to take a look.

To do

Think about each member of your family. What strengths, talents, or abilities have you inherited, acquired, or learned from them? For example, you may have inherited your father's good looks, acquired your mother's gentleness, and learned to make fine furniture from your brother. Use the space on pages 38 and 39 to record your thoughts. (Add additional family members on another sheet of paper if needed.)

Why do

Examining the sources of our strengths, talents, and abilities helps to build pride both in ourselves and our family.

Do

I have my: *strengths, talents, abilities, skills*

father's

_____

_____

_____

mother's

_____

_____

_____

brother's

name
_____

name
_____

sister's

name
_____

name
_____

More to do

What are some of the strengths, talents, abilities, and skills that members of your family have that you would like to develop, learn, or acquire?

I have my: **strengths, talents, abilities, skills**

grandfather's

father's side _____

_____

mother's side _____

_____

grandmother's

father's side _____

_____

mother's side _____

_____

other relatives

_____

_____

_____

_____

Life support

To

Help you
identify the people,
places,
and things
that give you
support,
nourishment,
and help you
grow.

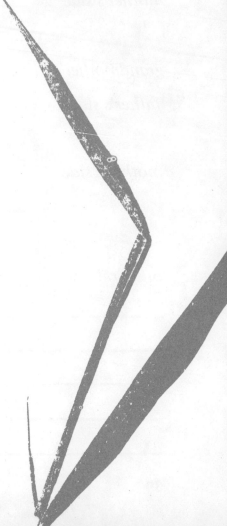

I simply can't stand this pond any longer," a frog told his friend one day. "It's too crowded for one thing, and too dull for another. There must be much better ponds nearby."

"Don't be too sure of that," said his friend. "We have lots of bugs to eat, nice lily pads to sit on, clean water, and plenty of places to hide from the fish. I'd want to be certain that another pond had as much to offer before I moved."

But the first frog hopped right up the bank and over the hills until he came to another pond. "This is more like it," he said and dove right in without looking up, down, right or left. He landed in the open mouth of a huge bass and was swallowed whole.

What is the moral of this tale?

a.

There's
no place
like home.

b.

Look before
you leap
or you will
make a bass
of yourself.

c.

Take stock
of all the
good things
you've got going
for you before
you throw them away.

To do

Think about the people, places, books, and ideas that have helped you grow. Who and what are they? What do they provide you? For example, your best friend may help to give you a feeling of courage; a book that you treasure may help to give you a sense of your own identity; a favorite spot may help you to relax and enjoy life. Use the space on pages 42 and 43 to write your responses.

Why do

When we identify the sources of our support and nourishment we are often better able to tap them when we need them. We also tend to better appreciate how we have become who we are as well as who and what has contributed to our growth.

Here are some things that people, places, books, and ideas may contribute to your growth:

courage	*friendship*
companionship	*joy*
security	*understanding*
identity	*love*
independence	*affection*
self-confidence	*recognition*
prestige	*self-fulfillment*
skill	*self-esteem*
wisdom	*safety*
knowledge	*inner harmony*
moral support	*happiness*

Do

people
groups/organizations

what they contribute

_____

_____

_____

_____

_____

_____

_____

_____

places   *what they contribute*

_____

_____

_____

_____

_____

_____

_____

More to do

What did you learn from this activity?   What are some additional sources of support   and nourishment that you might tap?

books   *what they contribute*

_____

_____

_____

_____

_____

_____

_____

ideas/other   *what they contribute*

_____

_____

_____

_____

_____

_____

Taking care of my needs

To

Help you get in touch with and take care of your present needs.

We learn in school that the basic human needs are food, clothing, and shelter. Yet you could have the most delicious of food, the most beautiful of clothes, and the most luxurious of homes and still be miserable and unhappy. For there is a vast group of other needs that must be met if we are to be happy, whole human beings—needs for love, recognition, self-respect, the feeling of belonging, a sense of accomplishment. Sometimes we have to pause in our pursuit of food, clothing, and shelter to take a look at these other needs.

To do

Make a list of things that you really like to do. (You can even include things that you have never done but would like to try.) Concentrate only on those things that make (or would make) you feel good and give you satisfaction. They can be such simple things as taking a long hot shower or such difficult things as climbing a high mountain. After writing your list in the spaces provided on page 46, go down the list and place a date beside each of the things listed to indicate when you last did them.

Why do

Identifying the things we like to do and then doing them can be an important first step in taking care of our very real needs for adventure, friendship, achievement, well-being, and self-fulfillment.

Do

things I like to do

when I last did it

day   month   year

More to do

Check your list and choose one or two things that you have not done for a while (or perhaps have never done) but which you would like to do soon and make a plan for doing them. If they are things you would like to do on a regular basis, such as, for example, playing tennis, make a schedule of your week's activities and find time to put them in. Then, try to stick to your weekly schedule. If something or someone should interfere, try to find a way to work it out so that you can keep to your plan.

WEEKLY ACTIVITY SCHEDULE

S	M	T	W	Th	F	S
Tennis		Tennis				

PEOPLE POWER

To

Help you identify the relationship between the people you spend time with and the degree to which these people contribute to your growth.

The poet John Donne said, "No man is an island, complete unto itself." And it is certainly true that we need other people in our lives as surely as we must have air to breathe. But just as there is more to life than breathing, there are some limits to the time you can give—or spend—to other people.

At first this may sound terribly selfish—and snobbish. But some people will gobble up all your time—talking, chatting about everything and nothing. We all need friends with whom we can relax, "let our hair down," and be ourselves. But we also need friends who challenge, compare, discuss, and encourage us whether by words or example, to try for bigger and better things. These friends may not always be so easy to be around. Yet sometimes even a few minutes spent with them provides food for thought and action for days to come. When you stop to think about it, all of us have only a certain amount of time to spend. It may be a mistake to let other people spend it for us as if it were their own.

To do

Make a list of the people you
spend time with each week.
Use the chart on the next page.
See the examples below.
On the average, how much time
per week do you spend with
each person? Enter the average
number of hours in column 2.
Then, rate each person in
terms of how much they
contribute to your growth by
placing an X at the
appropriate place on the scale.

Why do

When we become aware of the average amount
of time we spend with the people in our lives and
the degree to which they contribute to our growth,
we may be able to find ways to increase the
time spent with growthful people and decrease
the time spent with non-growthful people.

	average amount of time per week	Rating contributes very little or nothing				contributes a great deal
people						
Cindy Smith	4 hours	1	2	X	4	5
		1	2	3	4	5
		1	2	3	4	5
		1	2	3	4	5
		1	2	3	4	5
				3	4	5
						5

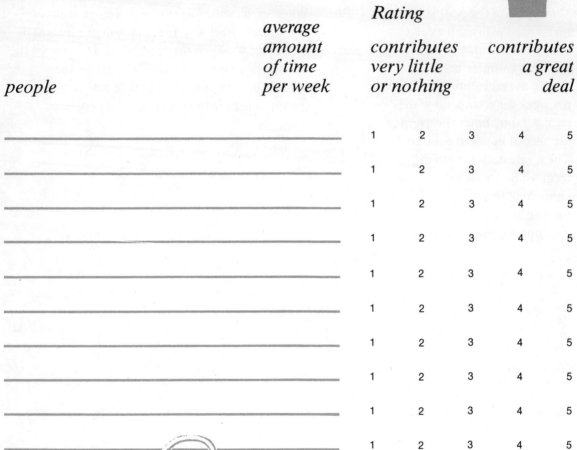

Do

people	average amount of time per week	Rating contributes very little or nothing				contributes a great deal
_____		1	2	3	4	5
_____		1	2	3	4	5
_____		1	2	3	4	5
_____		1	2	3	4	5
_____		1	2	3	4	5
_____		1	2	3	4	5
_____		1	2	3	4	5
_____		1	2	3	4	5
_____		1	2	3	4	5
_____		1	2	3	4	5

More to do

Look over your ratings. What are your findings? Are there any ways that you can increase the time you spend with people who contribute to your growth and decrease the amount of time you spend with people who do not contribute to your growth? List them below. Then, make a plan for doing something about it.

*ways to increase
the time spent
with growthful people*   *my plan of action*

_____

_____

_____

_____

_____

*ways to decrease
the time spent
with non-growthful people*   *my plan of action*

_____

_____

_____

_____

_____

TURNING POINTS

To

Help you identify the major turning points or critical past events in your life and who or what contributed to each event.

Sometimes it seems as if life unfolds like a drive through an unknown countryside without a road map. The scenery is pleasant enough but it soon gets monotonous until suddenly we come to a crossroad.

Which way to go? We take a turn and soon the landscape changes for the better or the worse. But far more important than a new view, each turning point means making a choice—a choice that will take you toward or away from where you want to go. Without a map it's almost impossible to make the right choice every time. But you can look back and see where you went wrong or right and construct a map of your life that may help you to take the right turn in the future.

To do

Think back over your life and identify at least five turning points or critical past events, which, if they had not occurred, would have made your present life much different. List them on pages 54 & 55. Then, identify the cause of the turning point or event in terms of whether it was internal (something within you which brought it about) or external (something beyond your initiation and control). Third, list the people involved. Finally, indicate whether the turning point had a positive or negative affect upon your life.

Why do

Identifying the turning points in our life, and who or what contributed to them, and what affect they have had on us can give us a better picture of whether we are in control of our own lives.

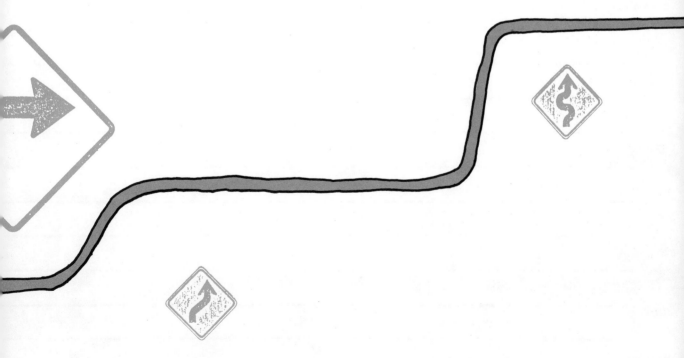

Do

turning points or
critical past events

cause
internal or external

More to do

Examine your responses at the left for patterns. Do you see any? What are they? What did you learn? Write some "I learned" statements by completing the sentence stem, "I learned that I. . ." several times.

people
involved

affect upon my life
positive or negative

_____

_____

_____

_____

_____

_____

_____

_____

_____

_____

_____

_____

_____

Guests of honor

To

Help you
get in touch
with some of
your values.

The waiters clear away the last of the dinner plates from the hundreds of tables. People settle back with cups of coffee and tea. The master of ceremonies rises and goes to the microphone in the center of the long head table.

"Ladies and gentlemen, I take great pleasure in presenting our very distinguished guests of honor. . . ."

You may never have an opportunity to honor your favorite people, or those you admire the most in such lavish fashion, but just suppose you could. Who would they be? And why is it that you admire them so much. If you knew, it might help you to become more like them.

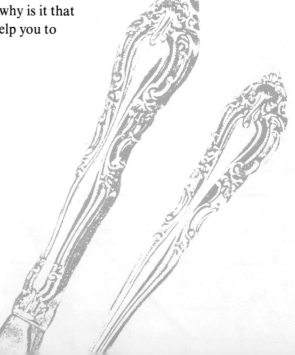

To do

You have decided to give a dinner party in honor of the five people you admire the most. Your first task is to identify the guests of honor. Make a list on page 58 of ten possible guests; they may be living or dead, famous or not, friends or non-acquaintances. Next to each name, indicate what you admire most about this person. Listed on page 58 are some admirable traits and characteristics you can use for thought starters. Then, narrow the list down to the five guests of honor you will invite.

Why do

If we identify
the people
we admire most,
our reasons
can help us
get in touch
with our values.

Do

courage
honesty
commitment
dedication
lovingness
reverence
independence

self-discipline
creativity
hard working
purity
power
intelligence
loyalty
caring

concern for others
orderliness
adventurous
perseverance
joyfulness
tenderness
wisdom

possible
guests

what I admire most
about this person

1. _____
2. _____
3. _____
4. _____
5. _____
6. _____
7. _____
8. _____
9. _____
10. _____

*final guest list
in order of preference*

1. _____

2. _____

3. _____

4. _____

5. _____

*alternates
in order of preference*

6. _____

7. _____

8. _____

9. _____

10. _____

More to do

Make a list of the people (friends, family, associates, etc.) you would like to invite to help you entertain your five guests of honor. What do you admire most about each of these people?

Sealed bid auction

To

Help you develop a priority ranking of your values.

When you go into a store to buy something, you expect and look for a price tag to be stamped or tied to the object. A can of peas costs so much, a pair of jeans costs so much—whatever. If the price seems too high you put it down and walk away to look for a better buy. But, in many parts of the world prices are not set so strictly. If a price is marked on an object, it is understood to be the amount to begin bargaining from. The buyer offers a far lower price—the seller comes down a little. The bids and offers continue until a final price is arrived at. In a really free market, things are worth only what you are willing to pay for them. An auction is the free market in action. A certain number of people compete to buy something at a price just a little higher than a rival bidder is willing to pay. Funny things happen at auctions, however. Some people place higher values on certain things than do others. Sometimes they end up paying far more for something that they could have purchased at a set price in any store in town. Sometimes they get great bargains. Auctions bring out not the basic costs of things, but the basic values people place on different things.

To do

On page 62 is a list of things which people spend most of their lives seeking. Look over the list. Which of these things is most important to you? Which is least important? Want to add items to the list?

Pretend that a sealed bid auction is going to be held. (In a sealed bid auction you are forced to bid without any knowledge of how others will bid. This is done by having each bidder place his or her bids in a sealed envelope. The person who bids the highest amount for any item gets that item.) You have $2,500 with which to bid. How will you bid? You may allocate your $2,500 in the manner you wish except there can be no equal bids—that is to say, you can not bid the same amount more than once. For example, you may bid $500 once but not again; that is, you may bid $499 or $501 but not $500. Make your bids on the next page.

Why do

When we know what our value priorities are, we are better able to set and achieve goals that are consistent with these values.

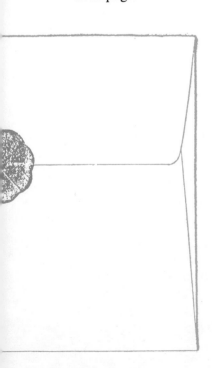

Do

your bid	*auction item*
_____	*500 acres of prime real estate in Florida*
_____	*A 4-year term as President of the United States*
_____	*Guaranteed fame as a movie star*
_____	*A love affair with the person of your choice*
_____	*A guarantee that for the next 30 years you will have excellent health*
_____	*Life after death*
_____	*A 1-2 year trip into the wilds of Africa or some other exciting place*
_____	*Five years of exhausting work culminating in the discovery of a cure for cancer*
_____	*A photographic memory*
_____	*A Guru with thousands of followers*
_____	*15 years to do whatever you want, whenever you want*
_____	*Plastic surgery and a new wardrobe to make you the most attractive person in the world*
_____	*Guaranteed success in the profession or occupation of your choice*
_____	*A home filled with happy children and a great deal of joy*

your bid	auction item
_____	*Many friends who consider you a significant person in their lives*
_____	*Winner of the Nobel Peace Prize*
_____	*Discovery of a truth serum which will wipe out myths and superstition*
_____	*Originator of a totally fair and just form of world government*
_____	*A chance to give 5 years of your life to a worthy cause*
_____	*A collection of the world's most beautiful paintings*

More to do

For the items above that you bid on, think about what value or values each represents. Write the value(s) in the margins next to each item. Here are some possible values that might be represented:

wealth	justice	salvation	harmony
equality	beauty	health	charity
security	friendship	tradition	knowledge
freedom	power	progress	wisdom
love	achievement	truth	family
peace	happiness	recognition	
	adventure	pleasure	

Now examine the values and bid items they represent. Are you happy with the bids you placed? Would you like to change any or leave them as they are? If you wish to make changes, note them here:

RESUMÉ

To

Help you develop
self-confidence
and feelings of
I-can-ness.

When a person sets out to find a job, or to change jobs, it is customary to prepare a brief listing of his or her skills, experience, and education—what level has been reached, what was studied, etc. Young people applying for a first job may find that they seem to have very little to list on this "resume" (rez-oo-may) or summing up of their lives to date. But it's good to sum up your life this way, nonetheless. You may discover more skills and positive accomplishments than you think you possess. And, you may discover some large gaps that you want to take positive action to fill in now.

To do

On page 66, write a resume of your past successes, achievements, and accomplishments from birth to present. The following are some things you might wish to include:

awards
honors
offices held
jobs you've held
things you've made
things you've written
things you've done
certificates you've earned
speeches
performances
grades you've earned
promotions you've made

Do

Resume for

name _____ *age* _____ *date* _____

Successes, achievements, accomplishments

age 1
to
age 10

_____

_____

_____

_____

_____

_____

age 11
to
age ____

_____

_____

_____

_____

_____

_____

Why do

The act of listing and reviewing our past successes, achievements, and accomplishments often serves to make us aware that we *can* do things, we *can* be successful, we *can* achieve. This realization or reconfirmation can help bolster feelings of self-confidence and I-can-ness.

More to do

Make a scrapbook which tells the story of your successes, achievements, and accomplishments. Use old snapshots, newspaper clippings, samples of your work, drawings, symbolic items, pictures from magazines which represent the event, and so on.

I wish I could

To

Help you identify
some of the
strengths,
talents,
and abilities
that you would
like to develop.

If you were given three wishes, what would the first one be? The best answer I ever heard to that age-old riddle is to wish for a thousand more wishes. That's the sort of thing that daydreams are made of. But wishes do come true. Not wishes for impossible treasure, sudden talent, beauty, or athletic ability, but wishes based on the reality of what is possible with patience and a little hard work. So wish away—and then work to make your wishes come true.

To do

In column one on page 70, make a list of some strengths, talents and abilities that you would presently like to develop. In column two, make some notes on what it would involve to develop the skill. For example, learning to play the piano would probably involve lessons (money) and a great deal of practice (time). In the third column, indicate how proficient you think you could become if you put your mind to it. In the last column, list your reasons for wishing to develop this skill or ability; what will you get out of it (pleasure, money, fame, etc.)?

Why do

Identifying strengths, talents, and abilities that we wish we could develop can help us set goals and grow toward our full potential.

Do

I wish
I could

Some ways
I could develop this skill,
ability, strength, etc.

More to do

Rank order your list from most important to least important. Place your rankings in the margins. Cross out any item(s) which you no longer wish to consider.

Degree of proficiency
low   high   *My motivation*

1 2 3 4 5   _____

1 2 3 4 5   _____

1 2 3 4 5   _____

1 2 3 4 5   _____

1 2 3 4 5   _____

1 2 3 4 5   _____

1 2 3 4 5   _____

1 2 3 4 5   _____

1 2 3 4 5   _____

1 2 3 4 5   _____

1 2 3 4 5   _____

1 2 3 4 5   _____

1 2 3 4 5   _____

1 2 3 4 5   _____

1 2 3 4 5   _____

1 2 3 4 5   _____

MOST RECENT ACCOMPLISHMENT

To

Help you develop an awareness that you can succeed, achieve, and accomplish things.

"**A**h, it was nothing!" is a reflex way to turn aside a compliment or congratulations on an outstanding play in a ball game, but the false humility bit can be overdone.

Too many people tend to put themselves down as a matter of habit. They forget their very real accomplishments because they are constantly measuring them against what seems to be the far more spectacular achievements of the famous, the brilliant, the rich, and the superstars. If you keep on saying that what you have learned, done, played, worked for, and accomplished is "nothing," you may soon begin to believe it. And, if you don't think your accomplishments are worth anything—who will?

To do

What is your most recent success, achievement, or accomplishment? It can be little, like learning a new card trick, or big, like getting a story published in a magazine. In the spaces on page 74 write about it.

Why do

By focusing on our most recent accomplishment, we often realize that we can and do achieve and succeed at things even if our successes are only little ones. The size really doesn't matter; the important thing is that we keep getting success feelings.

Do

My most recent success, achievement, or accomplishment was

_____

_____

_____

This is the way it happened

_____

_____

_____

This is who was there

_____

_____

_____

This is how I felt

_____

_____

_____

More to do

Pretend that you are a friend who cares very much about your accomplishments. Write a brief letter which praises your most recent accomplishment.

MY ACHIEVEMENT NEEDS AND MOTIVES

To

Help you identify your achievement needs and motives.

To do

List several of your achievements on the grid on page 76. (The more achievements you can identify, the clearer your picture of your achievement needs and motives will be.) Then check any or all of the boxes on the grid which apply. For example, if you did it partly or solely to earn money, check the first box in column 2 and so on.

Why do

When we are aware of our achievement needs and motives we become better able to direct our lives in more satisfying and successful ways.

Do

My past achievements	*I did it for the money and/or personal rewards involved.*	*I did it for the recognition and/or praise I would receive.*	*I did it for the fun and enjoyment involved.*	*I did it for the challenge and feeling of accomplishment involved.*	*I did it because I felt obligated, pressured, or forced to do it.*	*I did it to win; to be the best.*	*I did it so someone would like and/or accept me.*	*I did it for the friendship involved.*	*I did it to help or benefit someone else.*
rank									

More to do

When you finish, examine your grid. Do you see a pattern? What did you learn about your achievement needs and motives? What is your strongest need/motive? Which is least important? Rank order them in the space provided.

WINNER'S CUP

"It doesn't matter whether you win or lose. It's how you play the game." Do you believe that?

To

Help you develop feelings of pride and self-worth.

To do

You have just been notified that at the Winner's Circle Banquet, you will be awarded the WINNER'S CUP (a much sought after trophy in this country) for your five greatest successes, achievements, and/or accomplishments. Write them in on the cup on page 78.

Why do

Identifying and thinking about our greatest achievements can provide us with a sense of pride and self-worth.

Do

Winner's cup

presented to

_____

for

1. _____

2. _____

3. _____

4. _____

5. _____

More to do

Prepare your acceptance speech.

_____

_____

_____

_____

_____

_____

_____

_____

_____

_____

_____

_____

Future fantasy

To

Help you identify
some of the things
that you
would like to
achieve or
accomplish
in the future.

In a very funny short story, author James Thurber tells of "The Secret Life of Walter Mitty." Walter led the most ho-hum sort of everyday life but he was the world's champion day-dreamer. He imagined himself to be. . .a pirate, a famous surgeon, a rescuer of lovely damsels in distress—everyone and everywhere but where he was and what he was. Gradually his day dreams took over his life so that he spent more time in his fantasies than he did in reality.

There's a touch of Walter Mitty in us all, and it's a good thing to have fantasies, especially when you are young and there's still time to take some positive action and long-range plans to make at least one or two of them come true.

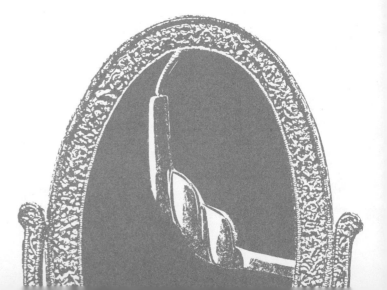

To do

Make a list on page 82 of some or as many of the things as you can think of that you would presently like to achieve or accomplish before you die. When you finish, think about the major skills or abilities that you would need to achieve or accomplish each one. Note these in the second column. To what degree do you already possess these skills and abilities? How confident are you that you could develop them? Check the appropriate response in columns 3 and 4 to answer these questions. Finally, think about the risks involved. Indicate your assessment in column 5.

Why do

Getting in touch with some of the things we would like to achieve, accomplish, or succeed at can help us identify more specific life goals.

Do

Desired achievements or accomplishments	Skills or abilities needed	I already possess these skills or abilities	I am confident I could develop these skills or abilities	low Degree of risk involved high
		YES NO	YES NO	1 2 3 4 5
		YES NO	YES NO	1 2 3 4 5
		YES NO	YES NO	1 2 3 4 5
		YES NO	YES NO	1 2 3 4 5
		YES NO	YES NO	1 2 3 4 5
		YES NO	YES NO	1 2 3 4 5
		YES NO	YES NO	1 2 3 4 5
		YES NO	YES NO	1 2 3 4 5
		YES NO	YES NO	1 2 3 4 5
		YES NO	YES NO	1 2 3 4 5

More to do

Examine your responses above. What do you see?
What did you learn?

My goals

To

Help you identify and clarify your goals.

To do

Complete the goals inventory below by listing your goals in each area. Then code the goals with the following symbols. Place them in the boxes next to the goal to which they apply. More than one code can be used per goal.

Why do

By developing an inventory of our goals we can get a clearer picture of which goals are the most important and least important to act upon.

1.
Place an ***** beside any goal which you have chosen of your own free will—that is, you do not feel pressured into setting this goal.

2.
Place an **R** beside any goal which involves risk (physical, psychological, financial, social, etc.)

3.
Place an **O** beside any goal which you have weighed both the positive and negative outcomes of achieving the goal.

4.
Place a **P** beside any goal which is a high priority goal.

5.
Rank order all of the goals which you have coded with **P**.

Do

My educational goals:

A

1. _____
2. _____
3. _____
4. _____
5. _____

B *My family-related goals:*

1. _____
2. _____
3. _____
4. _____
5. _____

C *My friendship goals:*

1. _____
2. _____
3. _____
4. _____
5. _____

D *My personal growth goals:*

1. _____
2. _____
3. _____
4. _____
5. _____

E *My career and work-related goals:*

1. _____
2. _____
3. _____
4. _____
5. _____

F *My leisure time goals:*

1. _____
2. _____
3. _____
4. _____
5. _____

G *My long-range life goal:*

1. _____
2. _____
3. _____
4. _____
5. _____

H *Other goals:*

1. _____
2. _____
3. _____
4. _____
5. _____

More to do

Write a future fantasy. Think about the kind of person you would like to be as well as the type of life-style you would like to be living 5–10 years from now. Be specific. What would you be doing? Where would it be? How would you be feeling? What would be the costs? What risks would be involved? Who would be there? What new skills and abilities would you need? What would you be doing during your leisure time?

When you finish your fantasy, compare it with the goals you have listed on the goals inventory. Will they help you achieve your fantasy? Are some of your goals taking you in a different direction? What goals would you have to add to realize your fantasy?

Making a plan to succeed

To

Help you organize
and make the
necessary plans
to act upon
and achieve
your goals.

To do

Choose a goal that you think you really want to achieve. Write
the goal in the space on page 88. Then complete the remainder of
the worksheet.

Why do

Setting a goal and achieving a goal are two different things. If we
hope to be successful in reaching our goals we must first be sure
that we are really committed to them, and then plan the
necessary steps to do the best we can to achieve them.

Do

1. List here the goal you wish to achieve:

_____

2. List some barriers which might prevent you from reaching your goal.
What are some steps you could take to overcome these barriers?

possible barriers   *steps to overcome barriers*

_____

_____

_____

3. Who are the people who might help you in reaching your goal?

name of person   *type of help he/she might give*

_____

_____

_____

4. How are your chances for success? What makes you think this?

_____

_____

5. What are some of the possible positive outcomes from achieving this goal?
What are some of the possible negative outcomes?

positive outcomes   *negative outcomes*

_____

_____

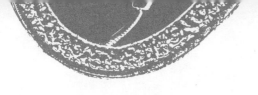

6. What are the chances that negative outcomes might occur? Can these odds be reduced? If so, how?

_____

_____

_____

_____

7. Do the possible positive outcomes outweigh the possible negative outcomes? Do you still want to try to achieve your goal?

_____

_____

_____

_____

8. If your answer is yes above, list the specific steps you plan to take to achieve your goal. If your answer is no, choose another goal and repeat the above steps. Steps I must take to achieve my goal:

_____

_____

_____

_____

_____

More to do

How do you feel about your plan? What are its strengths? What reservations do you have? Can you do anything to strengthen your plan?

_____

_____

_____

_____

_____

_____

_____

_____

_____

_____

_____

Signing a contract

To

Help you develop
a commitment
to carry out
your plan of action
and achieve
your goal.

con·tract: an agreement, especially a written one enforceable by law, between two or more people.

Webster's New World Dictionary

To do

Complete the self-contract on page 92 by writing in your name, the target date, the goal, the first step(s) you will take, and the date you will start in the appropriate spaces. Then, if you are sure that you will carry out the contract, sign it and get a witness to also sign it.

Why do

Making a contract with our self and getting it witnessed helps to build commitment and insure that we take action rather than procrastinate.

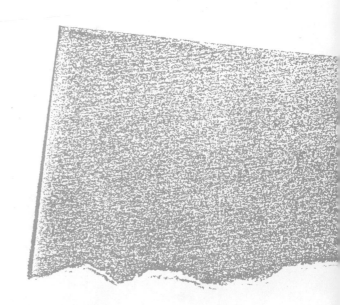

Do

A self-contract

I, _____, will by _____. As
   your full name   *date goal will be achieved*

achieve the goal of _____.
                    your goal

a first step I will _____.
                    your first step

I plan to take the first step by _____
                                 date

Signed _____ _____
       your signature   *date*

Witnessed by _____ _____
             signature of witness   *date*

More to do

Arrange to have the witness who signed your self-contract check back with you periodically to see how much progress you have made in completing your contract and achieving your goal.

arrangements made   *dates*

_____

_____

_____

_____

_____

_____

_____

_____

Making an assessment

When you've worked hard at learning and doing something it's not only satisfying, but necessary to know how good a job you've made of it. There's little satisfaction in simply going through the motions without measuring the results. They won't always be perfect the first time, or even the second. But it's better to know where you stand.

Pardon a personal note, but I have a friend who told me of his rather spine-tingling first drive with his son who had just gotten his beginner's permit. They had begun on quiet streets and then moved out onto a highway. The young driver did fairly well but tended to be a bit jerky and to drive, start, stop, and turn too fast.

"How do you think you did?" asked the somewhat shaken father when they finally pulled back into their home driveway.

"Just great," said the boy.

"How do you know?" asked the father.

"Because I missed every car we met," said the boy.

To

Help you evaluate the degree of success you achieved in reaching your goal and identify the factors which contributed to your success or failure.

To do

Complete the worksheet on pages 96 and 97.

Why do

Making an assessment of the things that contributed to our success or failure in achieving our goal can help us learn to be more effective in setting and achieving future goals.

Do

To what degree did you succeed at achieving the goal you set for yourself?

_____

_____

_____

_____

_____

_____

What things contributed to your success or failure in achieving your goal?

_____

_____

_____

_____

_____

_____

_____

If you were to do it all over again, what would you do differently, if anything?

More to do

How do you feel about the degree of success or failure you achieved? If your efforts were only partially successful or a complete disaster, can you think of any way that this can be turned to your advantage? What did you learn from your experience?

the me tree

To

Provide you
with a visual means
of recording
and assessing
your growth.

You've heard of "family trees"—the careful records which some people make of the names, dates, marriages, births, and deaths of their relatives as far back as they can go. The tree is a fitting symbol of such a history. Trees grow slowly, just as people do. You can count the rings in their trunks which mark yearly growth. Unfortunately, to do so you have to cut down the tree. So here is a special kind of tree that you can use for years without having to yell, "Timber!" Not a family tree but a ME TREE, designed for you to record your own record of growth as you *take charge of your life.*

To do

Step 1
Write your name on the trunk of the ME TREE on page 100.

Step 2
In the boxes attached to the roots of the ME TREE, write your strengths, talents, abilities and skills; one per box. Fill in as many boxes as you can. More boxes can be added if needed.

Step 3
In the circles attached to the branches of the tree, write your successes, achievements and accomplishments; one per circle. Fill in as many as you can. More circles can be added if needed.

Step 4
Keep your ME TREE in a handy place. Whenever you develop a new strength, talent, ability, or skill, add it to the tree. Likewise, whenever you succeed at, achieve, or accomplish something new, add it to your tree. Make your ME TREE grow as you grow by adding new roots and branches whenever you need them.

Why do

Keeping a visual record of our growth often provides us with an incentive to continually add to the record. As we see our ME TREE grow, it helps to build our feelings of self-confidence and self-worth.

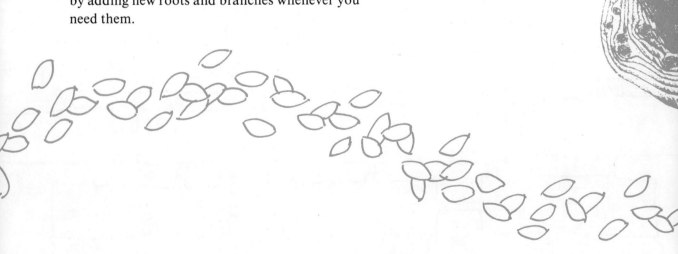

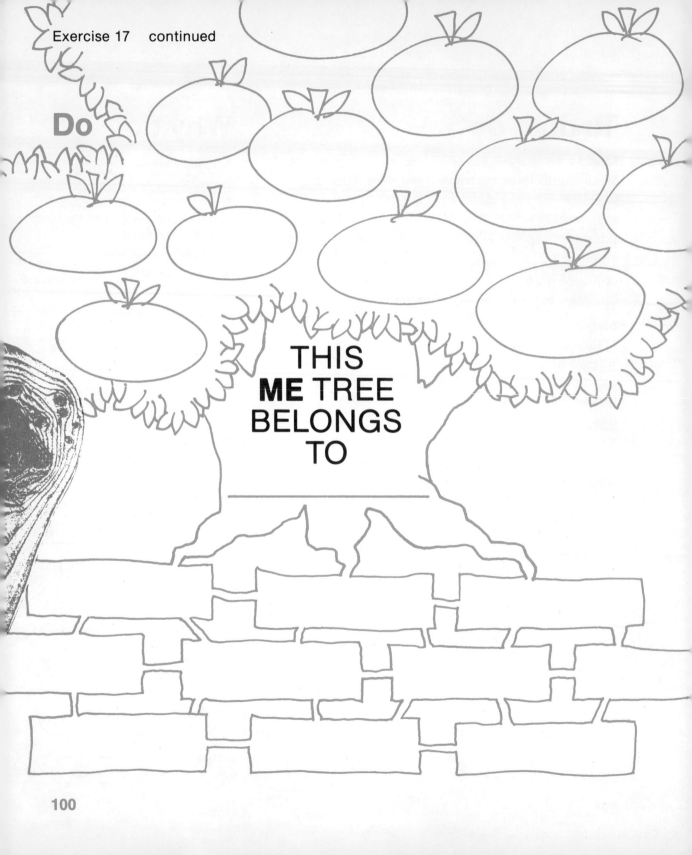

Do

THIS
ME TREE
BELONGS
TO

_____

More to do

Many of the goals we have do not lend themselves
to making elaborate plans of action. All we need to
do is to decide upon it and do it. For example, a
goal might be to read three very difficult books. For
someone who doesn't like to read, this might be
quite an achievement—something to be added to
the ME TREE. All we really have to do is decide to
do it and then do it. Below is a goal sheet which you
may find helpful for setting and achieving these
kinds of goals.

Each week (day or month) list a new goal for
yourself on the goal sheet, noting briefly the
specifics of how you intend to achieve the goal. At
the end of the week (day or month) write down the
results of your efforts in the space provided.

Goal sheet _____

name   *date started*

Goal for the week (day/month) of _____ *How I intend to achieve this goal:* *Results of my efforts:*	*Goal for the week (day/month) of* _____ *How I intend to achieve this goal:* *Results of my efforts:*
Goal for the week (day/month) of _____ *How I intend to achieve this goal:* *Results of my efforts:*	*Goal for the week (day/month) of* _____ *How I intend to achieve this goal:* *Results of my efforts:*
Goal for the week (day/month) of _____ *How I intend to achieve this goal:* *Results of my efforts:*	*Goal for the week (day/month) of* _____ *How I intend to achieve this goal:* *Results of my efforts:*

Dr. Leland Howe conducts workshops in values clarification in many major cities. If you would like to receive an announcement and be put on the mailing list, please send a self-addressed stamped #10 envelope to:

Dr. Leland W. Howe
Philadelphia Humanistic Education Center
8504 Germantown Avenue
Philadelphia PA   19118